Zeke Goes to Space School

Jill McDougall
Illustrated by Tom Bonson

Zeke lives on a planet far away.
It is his first day at Space School.

“I do not want to go,” said Zeke.
“I will not have any friends at Space School.”
“You will make friends soon,” said Mum.

"Here we are," said Mum.
"Space School will be fun."

“Come in, Zeke,” said Mr Moon.
“You will have fun here.”

“There are lots of things to do.”

Some aliens were playing with slime.

"Can I play?" asked Zeke.

"Yes," said the aliens.

Zeke took some slime. It was sticky!
“I do not like slime,” said Zeke.

Some aliens were playing with funny hats.
"Can I play?" asked Zeke.
"No," said the aliens. "There are no more hats."

Zeke felt sad.

He sat down on a rug.

“Hello!” said the rug.
“Oh!” said Zeke.
The rug was an alien!

“My name is Blip,” said the alien.
“Do you want to play with me?”
“Yes!” said Zeke.

Zeke and Blip made a rocket.

“Can we play?” asked some aliens.
“Yes!” said Zeke. “We can all fit in.”

Mum took Zeke home from school.
"Did you make a friend today?" she asked.
"Yes!" said Zeke. "I made *lots* of friends."